London's CITY BUSES

BARBRA'S HERE!
171A
Harringay Islington
Waterloo Camberwell
Greenwich Woolwich
ABBEY WOOD
WITH OMAR!
WLT 615

London's CITY BUSES

John A. Gray AM Inst TA

LONDON
IAN ALLAN LTD

First published 1979

ISBN 0 7110 0932 5

Published by Ian Allan Ltd, Shepperton, Surrey; and printed in the United Kingdom by Ian Allan Printing Ltd

---

Other books by the same author

London Buses in Camera
London's Suburban Buses

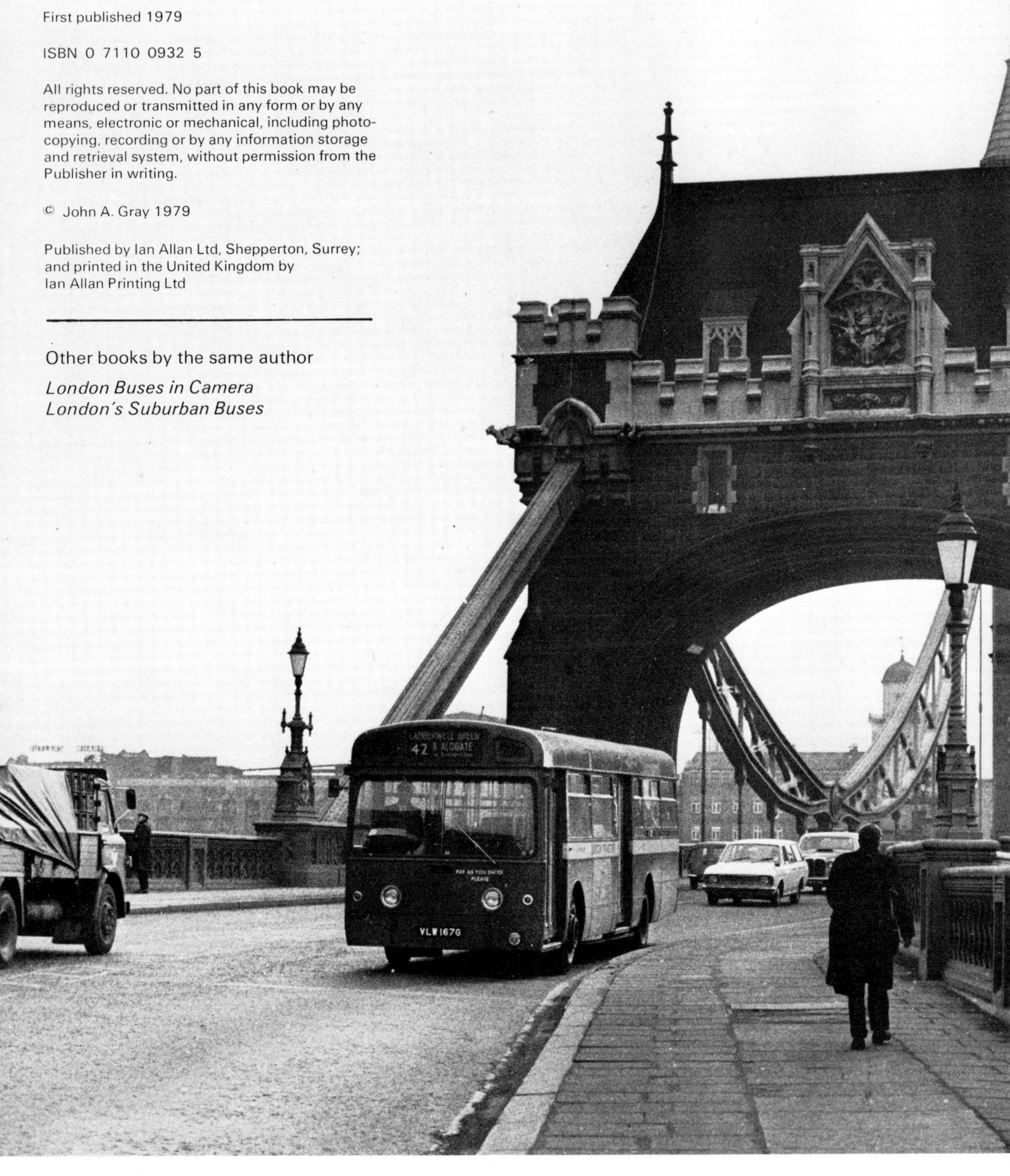

Contents

Half-title page: Routemaster — running to time? / *John A. Gray*

Title page: RM615 heads across Waterloo Bridge in Sunday afternoon sunshine early in 1969 on what must have then been one of the longest red bus routes, 171A. The pleasing architecture of Somerset House remains in the background. / *Edward Shirras*

Left: Route 42, one of the two routes to cross Tower Bridge, was traditionally operated with double-deck buses. It had a spell with a the long Merlin in use, as here with MB167 bound for Aldgate in February 1973. The bus, once an MBA Red Arrow, was taken out of LT's fleet four years later, when RTs more than twice its age remained very active. / *T. W. Moore*

Small layout, big day out
Red Bus
Rover
1,700 miles
£1.10p
11
ALDWYCH

Introduction

This book features buses and their operation within the three cities — London, Westminster and Southwark — that together form the core of Britain's metropolis. I have not forgotten that, strictly, Southwark was historically the first suburb of London, when habitation spread to the south bank of the Thames even before the walled London city was filled with buildings.

Westminster too was a suburb; the first westwards from the Romans' original London settlement. But these areas were almost entirely left out of *London's Suburban Buses*, and the present book therefore complements its predecessor. The West End, generally regarded as covering the nearest business and shopping areas to the City of London on its western side, is included here as well, to give a broad range of bus operation in the busiest area — in all senses — of London Transport's territory, from the 1933 unification to the present.

Acknowledgements

Much research was done in preparing this book and occasional conflicting evidence ensued. Verification at source has not always been possible in order to keep errors to a minimum. Contributors have given as much information as they could, frequently volunteering more than I've sought. All the information was both given and accepted in good faith as being accurate. Those errors that have not been caught in the net during compilation are my responsibility.

Though one or two corporate bodies have not felt able to give free help as before, all individual people have, and to them I am very grateful. Some people's help has been extremely valuable, and I mention them alphabetically now: Julian Bowden-Green; C. Carter; John Fielder; D. W. K. Jones; Tom W. Moore; Stanley A. Newman; George Robbins; John G. S. Smith; Colin Stannard, and my wife, Sandra.

Cambridge, June 1978 *John A. Gray*

Left: RM1606 on a Saturday short working of route 11 to Aldwych in April 1978 runs along the very short distance of Broad Sanctuary linking Parliament Square with Victoria Street. The architectural symmetry behind is the Methodist Central Hall. / *John A. Gray*

Liverpool Street

London's best known route is the number 11. Starting in Liverpool Street, immediately outside the ancient City of London, and to the north of it, the route runs through the heart of the City, then through the City of Westminster and on into the inner western suburbs. We can follow its course in picture, on a journey through the best known areas of Europe's largest capital city.

Liverpool Street panorama, early Saturday morning in April 1978. Routemaster RM409 lays over in front of a forlorn Broad Street railway station. / *John A. Gray*

Above: A three-axle AEC Renown of 1931 waits outside Broad Street station in early London Transport days to start a journey on route 11E, then the main service to Shepherds Bush. LT613 shows the straight staircase ascending past glazed lower-deck windows. / *J. F. Higham*

Centre left: In times of severe shortage of serviceable vehicles, London Transport has had to resort to borrowing vehicles from other concerns. This AEC Regent, borrowed for a while in the early wartime period, came from Leeds Corporation. It was Leeds' first Regent and carried a Roe 52-seat body. New in 1932, it was only a few years older than London's own equivalent, STL888 behind. / *G. Robbins collection*

Bottom left: This AEC Renown, LT1222, had an angled staircase unlit by side lower deck windows except for a lancet at the rear offside. A route number stencil showing white numerals cut out of a black metal slide usefully occupied the side panel. Bus crews chat to each other outside the then (1948) Underground station entrance as a Thornycroft Cygnet single-decker draws up behind. / *C. Carter*

Left: The roadsweeper has a friendly word with the driver of ST856 outside Broad Street station. The Tilling-built open staircase body shows the characteristic lower-deck sag that this make of bodywork suffered at the end of its working life. Had it not been for the war and subsequent delays in delivering new buses, this petrol-engined AEC short wheelbase Regent type would have been withdrawn from service well before this August 1948 photograph was taken. / *J. H. Aston*

Below: Travelling lady looks away from a Bristol hired before delivery to Southern National in 1949, another time when London Transport was short of buses. This one ran from Dalston garage; Hammersmith (later called Riverside) also ran hired Bristols on route 11 at the time. / *C. Carter*

Above: New Year's Day 1962 and snows falls on London. Eight-feet wide Leyland Titan RTW220 stands ready for the run to Dalston garage as a companion overtakes in beginning a slippery journey to Hammersmith.
/ C. Carter

Right: Beginning our pictorial journey through innermost London, round the corner on the same first day of 1962, in Finsbury Circus, is RT465. Here was the then terminus of route 133; snow has obliterated the bus's number indicator set into the roof.
/ C. Carter

City Streets

Streets in the City of London are constantly busy with traffic and people during the daytime, though there are less busy periods on Saturdays. On Sundays, sightseers replace the businessmen's demand and a rather different pattern of bus routes operates.

Even before the advent of the motor vehicle, the streets could not cope properly with all the traffic needing to use them; it was thought that by having underground railways, street traffic might be reduced. That solution to the problem failed: it encouraged more travel and traffic still, and the buses seemed to be just as much used. Progress through City streets on a bus can be irritatingly slow. Simply too many vehicles want to use the limited road space. More underground railways . . . ?

Minories, on the City of London's eastern flank, has only rear-engined Daimler Fleetline DMS321 to disturb its Saturday morning quiet in April 1978. The bus cuts a shaft of sunlight admitted by the Portsoken Street-Crosswall crossing. / *John A. Gray*

Top left: Wide Leyland Titan RTW352 on route 6A to Waterloo passes RM167 on 257 to Chingford Mount in Bishopsgate, August 1964. Four years later both routes were withdrawn (though 6A was used for a Saturdays only route via Bishopsgate to Oxford Circus). / *C. Carter*

Centre left: Early Saturday sunshine emphasises exhaust emission as two Routemasters pass in Bishopsgate in April 1978. RM729's long journey south to Bromley had begun at Shoreditch, less than a mile back; RML 2332's journey had started from London Bridge half a mile previously and still displayed as the destination. The longer Routemaster had only recently come into the LT fleet from London Country Bus Services, having been repainted — and no more — for LT service. / *John A. Gray*

Below: Going home. Bromley garage's STL175 indicates its home destination on route 47. A pedestrian hurries in front of this longer wheelbase AEC Regent, which dates from 1932, as it moves off in Gracechurch Street in about 1947. / *S. A. Newman*

Left: Again in Gracechurch Street, later-built STL1199 (but with intermediate bodywork style) was working from Camberwell garage on route 35 to Clapham Common. The route still goes there today, 30 or so years on. / *S. A. Newman*

Below: In the 1970s, early morning journeys have crossed the Thames at London Bridge to reach the City at Monument. Here, AEC Swift SMS336 stands near to where London's great fire began. / *D. M. Persson*

Above: The shell of Cannon Street railway station is the murky background for Metro-Cammell-bodied RTL942, resting at the terminus of tram replacement route 189A in May 1952. This route operated to this point on Saturdays only for quite a short period; introduced in January 1951, it ceased to reach Cannon Street station after October 1953. / *C. Carter*

Right: One of the first Daimler Fleetlines, DMS23, approaches Southwark Bridge after leaving Cannon Street station terminus. Its Park Royal standee bodywork shows the early arrangement of opening outwards upper deck front top windows; low sidelights at front, in line with headlamps; pay as you enter coin-in-slot symbols, and open relief bullseye symbol. For the first time, a production bus was in an all-over single colour livery of standard LT red, unrelieved by black wheel arch surrounds or white bands or window surrounds, as had been usual previously. / *J. G. S. Smith*

Above: A complete contrast to all-over red is given by this many-coloured mobile advertisement. In August 1971, RML2702 leaves the Bank of England and heads along Queen Victoria Street on route 15. / *C. Carter*

Right: On the opposite, eastern, side of the eight-road crossing at the Bank is Cornhill, the main east-west street through the central part of the City. Here, Leyland-built RTL1383 exchanges passengers one dull May day in 1964. Unusually, this bus had a roof-route number box body fitted on overhaul. / *C. Carter*

Right: Along the northern limits of the City runs London Wall, a street revitalised in the early 1960s. On 8 November 1961 — while office construction continued apace — RM939 celebrates the first day of buses along this new stretch of road, and the introduction of the new style route indicator blinds with capital initial and lower case letters for the placenames. / *C. Carter*

Below: Nearly 5,000 production AEC Regent Mk III RTs were made, and almost all of them were ordered by London Transport. Here the first of them, RT2, ascends Ludgate Hill towards St Paul's Cathedral on erstwhile route 96. The 56-seat bodywork was built by LT at its Chiswick works in 1939. / *C. Carter*

Above: At the same bomb-damaged spot in Ludgate Hill, all-Leyland-built STD57 dating from 1937 gets ready to pull up the hill. The appearance of these more or less standard Titan TD4 buses was superficially modified to resemble the current AEC Regent deliveries of the STL type, and their musically growling engine and transmission noises, heard often in provincial towns, were heard only in few parts of London where the 100 buses of this type, and another mechanically similar 11 which came during the war, were operated.
/ C. Carter

Left: Ludgate Hill in April 1978 and RML passes the uphill bus stop. This Routemaster is one of many to have been fitted with driver's two-way radio to link him with control staff. Only a slight protrusion in the front roofline (just discernible against the shaded backs of Farringdon Street premises) betrays the equipment.
/ John A. Gray

Right: Metro-Scania vehicles are made in Birmingham by Metro-Cammell, using Swedish-made Scania-Vabis engine, underframe and mechanical parts. 'Metropolitan' is the type name given to the rear-engined double-deck bus. MD44 displays the unusually deep nearside windscreen. Drivers' judgement of the nearside front corner is not so easy with a full-width front bus as with a half-width such as the Routemaster, and this deep window could be some help. The bus follows the line of the one-time Fleet ditch, now an underground sewer beneath Farringdon Street. The bridge in the background is Holborn Viaduct, built in the 1860s to span the Fleet, or Hole Bourne, valley. / *John A. Gray*

Below: The full load on DMS2475 — recently in service in this Spring 1978 picture — looks away from the Law Courts as the sightseeing tour passes Temple Bar, the entrance to the City of London from the Strand. The bus has the extended rear bulge to house its 'quiet' Leyland engine, with ventilation flues on either side. A Leyland nameplate is fixed above the more traditional Fleetline one. / *John A. Gray*

Kingsway and Aldwych

The king was Edward VII and the way was a new route through what had been a very densely populated and somewhat ill-famed area, to link two ancient routes, High Holborn and the Strand. A tram subway was built, as part of the scheme, beneath Kingsway from Aldwych to Southampton Row. It was opened in February 1906 for use by single-deck trams on a route to Bloomsbury. Within two years it was projected southwards beneath Aldwych on a twisty alignment to the Embankment. In 1930, the subway was closed for a year so that its floor could be lowered to permit the use of double-deck trams. It was reopened in January 1931.

The trams were withdrawn from the three routes using the subway in 1951 and 1952, and the replacing buses did not use it. The subway seemed to be closed for ever. But road traffic grew and congestion with it . . . and it was realised that the southern part of it could be made into that latest road engineers' device — an underpass. And single-deck Red Arrow buses were routed through the reopened stretch, for northbound traffic only, on the 501's introduction in 1968.

RM1900 on Saturdays and Sundays only route 77C heads south along Kingsway past the northbound (only) exit of the Aldwych underpass, formed by opening up the southern half of the old Kingsway tram subway. / *John A. Gray*

Top left: Nearly 30 years before, wartime-built Daimler D57 worked on route 77 in Kingsway. The bus had an AEC engine and Brush 56-seat bodywork. / *C. Carter*

Centre left: A prewar Bedford WTB coach, by now minus one headlamp, assists to give some sort of service on the close headway route 15 at Aldwych, in the 1948 period of LT's bus shortages. With label indicators obscuring the upper part of the windscreens, its driver would have had very restricted forward vision compared with today's standards. The coach firm, Eastern Belle, provided the driver and London Transport the conductor. / *J. F. Higham*

Below: Back at work for London Transport again! The first of LT's 20-seat Leyland Cub buses, C1, was new in 1934, with Chiswick-built bodywork and Leyland petrol engine with shallow radiator. In this picture it has the deeper radiator of the production batch. Though the LPTB's Cubs of this design did not work in Central London, C1 should have felt fairly at home even after sale by LT, in the red and cream of Overland Coaches, helping out in Kingsway. / *J. F. Higham*

Above: Clifton's TSM, new to Cronshaw Coaches some twelve years earlier, lends a hand on route 6 in 1949. Here in the company of an STL also on route 6, it takes a break at the Aldwych. / *D. W. K. Jones*

Left: How hard it rained on Coronation Day, 2 June 1953! Coloured stripes on the forward-facing lower deck front window denote the section of the Coronation Route RTL51 was serving on route 9. The destination displayed, Fair Cross LT Garage Only, is intriguing. Behind, the wider RTW overtakes another route 9 RTL standing at Aldwych's pavement. / *C. Carter*

Above: Aldwych, at the eastern side of London's theatreland, was the terminus for a short-lived special route called Starbus, running in one direction to Paddington station and calling only to pick up theatregoers on their homeward way to Park Lane car park and the station. DMS1301 shows the white stars on standard red livery used for the buses in 1972. / *J. G. S. Smith*

Left: Route 55 reaches Aldwych and, since 1978, Waterloo on Mondays to Fridays, and here in 1972, RT4627 was on duty. This elderly vehicle was still in LT's ownership at the time of writing. / *J. G. S. Smith*

Above: RM1533 passes Aldwych tube railway station, terminus of the shuttle train from Holborn running parallel to Kingsway. A Daimler follows behind, also on route 172, in this July 1976 scene. The route was one of two to replace the last of the Kingsway Subway trams in April 1952. / *C. Stannard*

Right: A Routemaster terminating on the 9 in April 1978 seems overawed by the dominating Bush House, the BBC's broadcasting colossus, in Aldwych seen from Kingsway. By this time, the fleetname on Routemasters had been all but entirely supplanted by the white roundel motif. / *John A. Gray*

Trafalgar Square and Charing Cross

In its centre, Nelson's column, flanked by Landseer's lions; all around, some of the best known streets and buildings in Westminster; but everywhere in Trafalgar Square there are people and pigeons vying for pavement space while buses circling clockwise between coming into and leaving the Square vie with other traffic for road space. Buses use seven of the eight streets opening into the Square; only Admiralty Arch has no regular service through it to The Mall. The spot marking Charing Cross lies in the south eastern corner; the name is generally applied to the immediate area, and buses use it in preference to Trafalgar Square on their indicators. Rare it is when no bus is in sight in Charing Cross or Trafalgar Square . . .

Continuing the route 11 theme, this Leyland open top bus was photographed in the Square in September 1933 soon after the London Passenger Transport Board took over London's bus services, though not all operators were taken over in one stroke. The driver of the Chocolate Express brown bus looks round to see if there are any more passengers for his fair weather bus at the stop outside St Martin's-in-the-Fields church. / *D. W. K. Jones*

Above: London weather, September 1972. Fleetline DMS128 picks a way through hurried movement in crossing the Square's north side to Duncannon Street. This bus shows the white relief between decks band the second delivery of Fleetlines had when new. / *T. W. Moore*

Left: RT3949 squeezes through traffic on the Charing Cross side of the Square in winter sunshine. / *J. G. S. Smith*

Above right: Wet shadows are cast by RT4292 as it enters Trafalgar Square from the north western side in 1972. Sometime later cars were banned from using the side of the Square on the left of this picture, to leave it more free for buses. / *T. W. Moore*

Right: The first Red Arrow bus route was started in April 1966 and its success encouraged more. Route 505, however, was less successful than some of the others, and it has been withdrawn since this 1972 picture. Unlike many of its type, Merlin bus MBA614 does survive; here its nearside windscreen wiper seems to be keeping the headlamp clean. / *T. W. Moore*

12
FOREST HILL
NLE 956
505 
WATERLOO STATION
RED ARROW
AML 614H
9
LIVERPOOL STREET
QUEEN ANNE SCOTCH WHISKY
ALD 961B

Left: Outside the National Gallery on the Square's north side, RT374 picks up on route 1 in 1948. The bus's Park Royal bodywork shows well the nearside front valence in line with the top of the windscreen; later RTs were built without this feature.

Below: Lights come on early in the evening rush in winter. RTs, RMLs and RMs were caught in the bustle of the north side in February 1973. */ T. W. Moore*

Left: Night time north side terminus. RM794 was picked out by the camera flash in September 1970 before leaving to go northwards. Well shown is the engine's radiator in its position out of line with the grille. The number-plate box has since been removed on many RMs, the plate being attached to the underside of the grille surround. / *Capital Transport*

Below: A rare daylight foray by a night bus. The eight blue and cream Leyland Cubs were used in innermost London on the Inter-Station route connecting main line railway stations during the evening and night; thus they were not seen very often in daytime. They had 18-seat Park Royal bodywork with a large space for luggage beneath the raised rear seats. This arrangement was adopted later for airport connection coaches, where passengers' observation from the raised deck would have been more effective than on a night journey between grimy London stations. / *J. F. Higham*

Top right: At the same spot on the Square's north side stands CR29, another Leyland Cub but this time with the engine placed at the back. Dating from 1939, the bus goes to show that there's nothing new in contemporary thought on positioning the engine. Some of these Chiswick-built 29-seat buses were used on red route relief work in the desperate days of 1946. / *J. F. Higham*

Centre right: In 1939, one of the private hire batch of Leyland FEC underfloor-engined coaches, TF2, collects in Cockspur Street for the short-lived Seeing London Tour. The war was to stop the tours very soon afterwards. The bodywork design is very similar in principle to the CR though the latter was both lower and shorter. TF2 was one of the 11 of the 12-strong private hire TFs to be lost by bombing during the war. / *D. W. K. Jones*

Below: Hello there! A rare chance to see London — no doubt looking more grey than ever through darkened windows — from a native USA-registered Allison 'turbo-powered Americruiser' three-axled coach as, in its rainbow livery, it enters Charing Cross from the eastern side of the Square in April 1978. Both the statue and the pigeon feeding crowd have their minds elsewhere as this extremely un-London like vehicle passes them by. / *John A. Gray*

Above: No one need queue, as exhorted, for elderly RT4630, by April 1978 working as a driver training bus from Plumstead garage. Charing Cross (Queen Eleanor's Cross) once stood about here — its Victorian replacement stands in front of the railway station — and was the point whence mileages from London were measured. / *John A. Gray*

Right: Policeman on horse and RM130 wait in Charing Cross for the traffic lights to change to admit them to the southern side of the square in Spring 1978. The bus retains the ventilation louvres above the openable upper front windows; when new, the bodywork had large fixed panes here. / *John A. Gray*

Left: The lion seems to contemplate a Routemaster's comparable solidity. RM594, in June 1977 at Charing Cross, carries the early style body with fixed upper deck front windows built for the first 240-odd buses in the class; it would have been changed at overhaul. / *C. Stannard*

Below: At Charing Cross nearly 30 years earlier, STD38 on the long-established route 13 chases STL1080 on the now defunct route 60. Both buses have the first postwar livery which included a light brown roof as well as two large areas of white, black wings and reddish brown wheels. / *J. F. Higham*

Above: Will this be London's bus of the future? After some disappointing experiences with types delivered since Routemaster days, London Transport tries one of the British Leyland group's prototype B15 rear-engined buses, pictured here in May 1977 at Charing Cross. Seating a total of 71 passengers and featuring full depth lower deck windows, the type has been given the revived name 'Titan'. / *C. Stannard*

Right: This Daimler Fleetline displays the later front lamps arrangement provided from DMS168 onwards. One-man-operated DMS402 enters Charing Cross on the south side of Trafalgar Square from Whitehall in August 1972. / *Capital Transport*

Above: Metro-Scania MD138 leaves Whitehall to its sister bus following and turns into Charing Cross in July 1977. The thick aluminium beading below the lower deck windows helps to improve the appearance. / *T. W. Moore*

Right: Nelson aloft another old timer! This AEC Regent, ST922, was restored some years ago and, though privately-owned, has been used on special route 100 (the number was luckily vacant) for several years in the 1970s. / *T. W. Moore*

Left: No excuse is needed to include a second view of ST922 as it pulls away from Charing Cross in July 1977. The conductor ascends the outside staircase to issue Bell Punch tickets to outside passengers — for the top deck in open-top buses was outside compared with inside for the lower deck, or saloon — some of whom perhaps are reminiscing on bygone days when similar petrol-engined buses carried them routinely on London journeys. / *T. W. Moore*

Ashby & Horner
TOWER OF LONDON 100
STRAND (LAW COURTS)
ST PAUL'S CATHEDRAL
MONUMENT
Burberrys
BRO 531 F
GJ 2098

Right: Back to the north eastern side of the Square to welcome MD117 entering from Pall Mall in 1977. All buses of this type are worked by a two-member crew. / *T. W. Moore*

Below: The Ionic columns of Canada House turn the eye from Trafalgar Square to Pall Mall as five members of the Routemaster family approach in September 1972. Nearest is RML2393 whose tyre marks show its turn from the Square's western side. / *T. W. Moore*

Whitehall

Replacing the River Thames link between the City of London and the seat of Parliament at Westminster, Whitehall as a thoroughfare was the predictable place to site Government offices as they became necessary. Several of the earliest London motor bus routes still ply its length, supplemented by later comers in tram replacement buses, though the trams themselves ran along the roughly parallel Victoria Embankment rather than Whitehall.

Picking up our route 11 again, here is single-deck AEC Renown LT1128 in rebuilt form helping out in postwar shortages. / *S. A. Newman collection*

Above: Another Renown, this time with the shorter wheelbase for the double-deck version, at the same place, in June 1953. By this time the bus had been cut down and converted into a tender for handling bus stop shelters. The vehicle had been LT951, one of the 'Bluebird' variety. RTL936 leaves space to pull out from behind. / *D. W. K. Jones*

Right: Coming much nearer the present, RCL2236 is driven by a trainee past the War Office in April 1978. A one-time Green Line coach, this long Routemaster remained in London Country Bus Services' livery though sold to London Transport, which simply applied the white bullseye motif. / *John A. Gray*

Above : In October 1950, new bus route 170 largely replaced Kingsway subway tram route 31. Twenty-three years later, a one-man bus with a passenger capacity similar to a tram's, DMS118, heads north along Whitehall to its usual shortened terminus at the Aldwych. / *T. W. Moore*

Right: Wintry Whitehall. RT3925 on the very long route 12 blinks left as it collects passengers well clothed against the February 1973 cold. Several of the longer routes in London are worked in two overlapping sections, to minimise the effects of traffic delay; route 12 has been worked this way for very many years. / *T. W. Moore*

Left: This RT, 219, was one of the lowest-numbered still to remain in service when photographed in August 1977. The elderly persons referred to in the advertisement were nearly 30 years younger when this bus was new. It was helping out on the long 29 route; Routemasters — one is following — were customarily working the route then. / *C. Stannard*

Below: An early postwar panorama of the Cenotaph area of Whitehall shows utility Daimler D28 with its ribbed-roof Duple bodywork travelling southwards on one of the 77 group of routes as STLs — still with their wartime white discs painted on the lower back ends — pass towards Charing Cross.

Above: At the time when gold transfer fleetnames and numbers had been almost completely supplanted by white roundels and numbers for all but the oldest members of the operational fleet, RM1533 still has gold fleet numbers in April 1978 though sporting roundels. The bus is passing the Cenotaph and the Foreign & Commonwealth Office. / *John A. Gray*

Left: As an RT speeds past the Foreign Office, STL1218 stops well away from the kerb for passengers to alight. With unique index letters in its registration for a London bus, it was also unusual in having the later style bodywork. / *S. A. Newman collection*

Above: King Charles Street is less famous than, but runs parallel to, Downing Street and it was here that former London buses RT1969 and MB638 had been parked, apparently to dispense refreshments to visiting film crews. Both vehicles, painted light blue, bore the legend 'Location Facilities Ltd' in rustic lettering, and the MB even had gold fleet numbers applied: April 1978. / *John A. Gray*

Right: Towards it southern end, Whitehall becomes Parliament Street, whose width is demonstrated by three Routemasters in July 1977. RM1746 on route 3 pulls out past coincidentally immediate fellow RM1747 on the 11, with passengers alighting, as RM454 collects travellers from the pavement. / *T. W. Moore*

Above: When route 163 took over from the trams in July 1952, it started from Horse Guards Avenue off Whitehall and was worked partly by STLs. In January 1965 it was extended well north of Whitehall to the southern slopes of Highgate, ironically, Parliament Hill Fields. Waiting to enter the corner of Parliament Square, RT2327 was caught in Parliament Street subsequently, before the route's demise in January 1970. / *Edward Shirras*

Centre right: No London bus this, but a former motorway coach originally in the Standerwick fleet of Ribble Motor Services. This Bristol VRL extra long vehicle has its length emphasised by the orange and white livery, here in Parliament Street in spring 1978. Coaches of this type have been used on London sightseeing tours by independent operators. / *John A. Gray*

Bottom right: Let's turn the clock back to 1935 to recapture this scene in Great Scotland Yard. T363 was an AEC Regal acquired by the Country Department with the services of Lewis Omnibus, Watford, a Metropolitan Railway associate, and was handsomely bodied with hinged doors back and front. With a Leyland Tiger for company it waits on a private hire duty. / *D. W. K. Jones*

Parliament Square and Westminster Bridge

Westminster — not the City of London — is the seat of Britain's government and Bridge Street, in the shadow of the Houses of Parliament, once the Palace of Westminster, seems to be the constantly hectic heart of Westminster, linking the Bridge with Parliament Square. Though trams crossed this Westminster Bridge (the second on the site, built in the early 1860s), none traversed Bridge Street: they all went along the Victoria Embankment.

As a giant traffic roundabout, Parliament Square has only rare moments in the daytime without any buses circulating it, although buses from Bridge Street bound for Whitehall are now excused the circumnavigation and there are exceptions when, usually with Whitehall, it is closed temporarily for State occasions.

Twenty-five Routemasters gained a silver livery with red band for Queen Elizabeth's Silver Jubilee Year. SRM14, otherwise RM1896 (with Leyland engine) was operating on route 11 in the May. / *C. Stannard*

Left: Passing roadworks on Westminster Bridge, Merlin MBA614 works on one of the Red Arrow routes linking the main line railway stations, Victoria and Waterloo, in February 1973, with a background that is one of London's best known.
/ *T. W. Moore*

Below: Two RTLs cross the bridge amidst dense traffic in the mid-1950s. Leading RTL236 had been sold by early 1959; following RTL1538 was sold even earlier; in 1958 it went to Ceylon. Descendants of the 59/159 family of routes still operate today, though on a reduced scale. / *Don Morris*

Above: Let's turn the clock back to those prewar days when three men could form a private hire coach crew. Proudly they pose in Parliament Square with their Daimler steed, DST6. It was a Daimler CH6 type new in 1931 to West London Coaches for its London-Amersham-Aylesbury coach service and was disposed of by 1938. Here it carried dual fleetnames 'Green Line' in smaller lettering above 'London Transport'. / *D. W. K. Jones*

Right: LTC14c waits patiently in 1938 on a private hire duty outside the Palace of Westminster. The 24 members of this type were based on the AEC Renown chassis and had petrol engines when new in 1937 and preselective gearboxes. / *D. W. K. Jones*

Above: In 1946 the diminutive CRs were pressed into relief work after wartime storage. The passenger in the doorway of CR19 could hardly have been deafened by the rear Leyland engine as the bus, on route 88, turns from Parliament Square. / *S. A. Newman*

Right: A run on the Round London Sightseeing Tour makes a contrast for the solitary rear-engined Routemaster FRM1 in February 1978 after its previous shuttling at Potters Bar. Entering the Square from Bridge Street, the bus has a familiar appearance due to much use of standard Routemaster bodywork parts. / *Julian Bowden-Green*

red bus rovers
12
Oxford Cir Whitehall
Elephant Camberwell
Peckham Forest Hill
red bus rovers
DULWICH PLOUGH
WLT 310
12

Left: Leaving Bridge Street behind, RM310 mounts Westminster Bridge in February 1973 with a predating RT passing the opposite way alongside the Palace of Westminster on the same route. / *T. W. Moore*

Right: Not a London Transport bus, but a type often seen and infrequently portrayed, this Metropolitan Police bus, based on the Bedford VAS chassis, leaves Parliament Square for Victoria Street in the late spring of 1978. Its bodywork is painted Lincoln green with a silver roof. / *John A. Gray*

Below: Pointing towards Victoria, though not reaching it on route 88, RT1634 and RM1598 run in tandem along Victoria Street from Parliament Square before turning left into Marsham Street. This RT had a 25-year life before going for scrap in August 1976. / *J. G. S. Smith*

Victoria's Buses

Victoria is a district named after a Queen and having buildings mostly erected there during her reign. It is also the name of three railway stations, though for 56 years now the two main line terminals have been treated at least in principle, as one. The third is the Underground station, and between them is London's best-known bus station, whose raisons d'être are much photographed, even though the roof now covering it precludes much camera work. No excuse is proffered for including a large selection now.

Below left: On the way to Victoria we could deviate to LT's head office at the Broadway, Westminster. Displayed for inspection there in 1936 was the first rear-engined Leyland Cub with the more usual version in C6B close behind for comparison. CR1 seems to have no fleet number applied yet; it carried a Leavesden Road, Watford, garage running plate. / *D. W. K. Jones*

Right: This former Overground company Dennis Lance had been repainted into LPTB livery and given fleet number D9 by September 1933. It displays the General fleetname, used at first by LT. It shares a stand in Victoria with a Chocolate Express Leyland Titan which was to pass to London Transport with the business and become TD101. / *D. W. K. Jones*

Below: Welcome to Victoria station in 1937 — arriving by Imperial Airways' AEC coaches (operated on contract by Thomas Tilling) after the drive from Croydon airport. The bus station, like an airport, had a control tower too. / *D. W. K. Jones*

Left: STL1262 takes a lay over on route 16 at Victoria bus station during the war. The bus had one of four new shortened STL chassis built in 1936 to accept bodies from Daimler CH6 chassis of LPTB and its constituents. Three off LGOC Daimlers had standard ST bodies but this one came off a Redline CH6 and was built by Christopher Dodson. Scrapped in 1944, the body was then replaced by a spare ST one.
/ G. Robbins collection

Below: The first 150 double-deck AEC Renowns had open staircase bodies. LT118 in early postwar days shows its fleet number painted white on the rear roof dome. Buses at a few garages were so equipped to help with fuel recording.
/ S. A. Newman collection

Left: All LTs after 151 had enclosed staircases, and the next main batch of almost 800 were of the general style LT491 exemplifies here, though there were several arrangements for indicators. The shaped white projection central from the upper deck front windows held a lamp to light a one-time hand painted route board above the indicator box.
/ *Lens of Sutton*

Below: Another variant with three boxes, LT177, gives the opportunity for conflicting displays with only two boxes available!
/ *S. A. Newman collection*

Right: LT439, also from Leyton garage, begins to show signs of sagging with wear and age after a busy life. / *Lens of Sutton*

Below: 'Bluebird' was a nickname applied to the last main design of double-deck LT buses, whose front upper decks were jettied in front of the driver's cab. This and an angled staircase allowed room for four more seats so that the bus's capacity became 60. LT1261 runs in Grosvenor Gardens on final approaches to the bus station. / *S. A. Newman collection*

Above: It must have seemed strange to see a single deck bus at Victoria in about 1950, when no 'little-ones' normally ran in the heart of London. Single-deck routes were then still reckoned to be numbered in the 200 series. LT1112 provided the unexpected, standing outside the Edwardian façade of the old South Eastern & Chatham Railway station. / *Lens of Sutton*

Left: ST9 was one of a few STs to emulate one of the LT's frontal styles. The lady could easily engage the driver's attention as the cab entrance was quite open, without any door. / *S. A. Newman collection*

Left: The most familiar style of the short Regent is provided by ST433, leaving Grosvenor Gardens in company with SRT69 in about 1950. / *Lens of Sutton*

Below: The straight dash and square cab corner STs with the high fleet numbers came into the LPTB from a major country area constituent, the East Surrey Traction Co Ltd. ST1128 (Ransomes' bodywork) is so close behind another route 38 bus that its Surrey registration mark (PG7993) is obliterated. / *S. A. Newman*

Right: Curved back STLs and straight back ST display their wartime warpaint: brown roofs; white discs, platform steps and back wall bases. In the early days of the war, fully-detailed route information continued to be displayed, and the glass anti-splinter mesh had still to be applied to the windows. / *G. Robbins collection*

Below: right: Postwar now and RT183 edges into the scene dominated by STLs 784, 1338 and 621 and watched by an inspector's keen eye. / *B. T. Cooke*

29
SOUTHGATE
DUNLOP
the ONLY TYRES with TEETH
GROSVENOR Pl HYDE Pk Cnr
PARK LANE MARBLE ARCH
EDGWARE Rd MAIDA VALE
KILBURN HIGH RD
SHOOT UP HILL
16
CRICKLEWOOD
Craven 'A'
WILLS'S
GOLD FLAKE
DLU
248
DUNLOP
the ONLY TYRES with TEETH
38 CHINGFORD
GOLD FLAKE

CHINGFORD
38
16
CRICKLEWOOD
52
LADBROKE GROVE
BXD 429
CLX 525
AYV 771

Craven
OUGHTON STN
SLINGTON WOODFORD
38A
LONDON TRANSPORT
HLW 71 
16
CRICKLEWOOD
VINEYS
COACHES
Vineys
LEYLAND
WG 1276
EYE 592

Above left: To help fill the urgent need for new buses at the end of the war, Leyland obliged with 65 double-deck buses built throughout by the firm. A few concessions were made to LPTB, such as the provision of a three-piece front route information display, although STD142 used only part of the largest one. Towards the end of their short London life in 1955, some had the full display treatment. There was no provision made for display at the back. / *S. A. Newman collection*

Left: The drivers seem to be commiserating, perhaps about their respective coaches, resting at the bus station while on hire to LT in 1948. The ex-Alexander Wycombe-bodied Gilford 168OT on the left displays 'Elms, Phillips & Brown' its owner in its destination box, but no route details, merely an 'on hire' sticker. Vineys' Leyland Tiger in prewar days was with Medway Transport, Gillingham. Here, with built up wings and a band securing the starting handle from the headlamp stem, it shows route 29 termini. / *S. A. Newman collection*

Above: One of Grey-Green's Bedford OB/Duple 29-seat coaches adds an element of gracious style to travel on route 76 in 1948; Park Royal-bodied wartime Guy G7, behind, would have given a distinctly less comfortable ride over the same route. / *J. F. Higham*

Right: The first of thousands. RT152 at the time of entering service in 1947 showed a large all-round improvement over the old LTs. / *S. A. Newman collection*

Right: RT187 on route 38 meets half sister SRTs on the 16. By 1949, RT family bodywork manufacture was running ahead of chassis output, and so plans were laid to rebuild and adapt 300 STL chassis to take RT bodywork. Only 160 were turned out. They retained the STL's mechanical features. Here's SRT86 in 1953.
/ C. Carter

Below: Who fancies Ferndale for a ride to the further East End? Many did in 1949 when this hired AEC Regal helped move a queue in the homeward evening rush.
/ D. W. K. Jones

Left: RT1463 stands before buildings catering to the traveller — the Shakespeare public house and Stewarts' wellknown restaurant — in the mid-1950s. Two batches of RT bodies were orderd from unexpected builders in 1948: Saunders Engineering and Cravens of Sheffield, perhaps explaining why bodies ran ahead of chassis production to give rise to the SRTs. The Cravens' version, exemplified here, was distinguishable by its five main bays' construction (four in standard RTs), a curved back and shallower upper deck front windows. / *Don Morris*

Below: Routemasters were gradually introduced to more routes in the 1960s, often at weekends only at first. RMs 1716 and 1794 are pictured at their Victoria terminus in Vauxhall Bridge Road shortly after their Saturdays introduction to route 181. RM1716 on the left has the lower part of the heater intake panelled over to permit a continuous light band, whereas RM1794 has the original full intake grille, but later style separate registration numberplate. / *Edward Shirras*

Right: Unusually, an AEC Swift works on a Red Arrow route. SMS330 was photographed in 1972 on the short-lived (July to October) and short distance (bus station to Victoria coach station) route 511, with black on white indicators. The route was operated only at weekends.
/ *J. G. S. Smith*

Below: By February 1977, MBA461 had a London Transport fleetname rather than 'Red Arrow' as it circuited Victoria on the since-withdrawn 506.
/ *Julian Bowden-Green*

Right: RT1706 helps out on route 38 in the winter of 1977, working from Clapton garage. As if to prove allegiance to Routemasters, it uses RM blinds front and side.
/ Julian Bowden-Green

Below: London Transport hires again! OM7, here in Grosvenor Gardens in May 1976, was the last of seven former Birmingham & Midland Motor Omnibus Co (Midland Red) owned and built buses bought by Obsolete Fleet Ltd and hired to LT expressly for the Round London Sightseeing Tour, which they worked in the seasons 1975-77. The D9 type, as Midland Red called it, was a chassisless bus and had a direct selection epicyclic gearbox, operated hydraulically. The Metal Sections-framed bodywork held 72 passengers within a 30ft length; the capacity was reduced by two on conversion to open top. The design makes an interesting comparison with its London contemporary, the Routemaster.
/ C. Stannard

Above: Leyton garage's RML2702 visited route 38 in February 1978. / *Julian Bowden-Green*

Left: More expectedly, a roundly 26½ft long Routemaster on the 38. RM1904 has the company of DMS320 beneath the 'Victoria Bus' headline in April 1978. / *John A. Gray*

Above right: Sunlight and shadow in spring 1978. Beautifully detailed railway station verandah looms behind DMS833 on route 10, whose side destination indicator is out of use, and RM676, where conductors chat at the open platform. / *John A. Gray*

Right: Utility without grace: the bus station shed shields 1978 sunshine from fictitiously destined RM2165 on route 52. A passenger boards MBA538 for a Red Arrow ride for West End shopping, while DM928 offers alternative shopping in a less traditional manner at the 16A's Brent Cross destination. / *John A. Gray*

SANYO
at the touch of a
YOUR UNION
52

4
38
WORK IN BANKING IN FINANCE?
52
BAKER STREET STN
YOUR UNION
CUV 165C
3
52
500 VICTORIA STATION & OXFORD STREET
VLW 538G
2
500
16A
SMU 928 N
1
16
UNDERGROUND

Above: Power at the back, demonstrated by Metro-Scania MD3 (left) and Metro-Cammell-bodied DMS2001 pointing towards Victoria Palace theatre. / *John A. Gray*

Right: When running in a bus lane against a one-way street flow, bus headlamps should be alight. RM1816's were still ablaze after having left Buckingham Palace Road's bus lane, here passing the terminating RM1938 on route 11 outside the Underground station in April 1978. / *John A. Gray*

Left: STL2477 had a unique body and always seemed to work from Alperton garage. Here it was a little off course, at Victoria's Gillingham Street garage, and out of service. / *S. A. Newman collection*

Below: The end of the line for STL16 as a trainer bus, on Gillingham Street's hard standing. These upright STLs always kept their petrol engines; many other types so equipped when new were later changed to diesel. / *S. A. Newman collection*

Victoria's Coaches

Coaches have always tended to centre on Victoria, essentially a Victoria different from the world of railway stations, an area west and south from them, in Buckingham Palace Road and some streets leading off. The purpose-built provincial coach station in Elizabeth Street which succeeded one in Lupus Street, Pimlico, is omitted from this selection; 'coaches' in this chapter refers to the Green Line variety. The quantity now is much reduced, caused by route withdrawal and service reductions. Eccleston Bridge has little room for Green Lines to stand; its one-way flow does not permit.

The once familiar prewar AEC Regal coach formed the backbone of Green Line services both sides of the war. T622, already full, still has a queue waiting anxiously in postwar days on Eccleston Bridge for a trip into Kent, although mostly through Surrey. / *S. A. Newman collection*

Above: Relieving on route 708, country area bus Q56 has a full complement too. This type of bodywork, dating from 1935/6 had an array of window shapes compared with today's standard. It was built by the Birmingham Railway Carriage & Wagon Co on AEC Q type chassis whose engine was mounted offside behind the front wheels.
/ S. A. Newman collection

Right: Also relieving on 708, East Grinstead garage's standard STL1479 moves smartly along. Until the RT was introduced, LT's prewar double-deck buses had no door to the driver's cab.
/ S. A. Newman collection

Above: RTC1 was very much rebuilt from RT97 after a postwar pay-as-you-board experiment was proved unsuccessful. It had a short Green Line life, mostly due to several novel features which turned out to be unsatisfactory in service. Though the coach retained the front engine, the radiator was repositioned beneath the staircase and coupled with a saloon air conditioning and heating system. The rebuilt vehicle emerged from secrecy at Chiswick in April 1949, with seating for a mere 46 passengers. Elusive to photograph in Green Line service, it was caught here turning out of Buckingham Palace Road on to Eccleston Bridge, Victoria on route 704. */ S. A. Newman collection*

Left: One of the 15 eight-feet wide AEC Regal Mark IVs with Eastern Coach Works 39-seat bodies introduced in 1951 stands in Belgravia. RFW3 gave a very comfortable ride, as intended for its private hire work. */ S. A. Newman*

Top right: An inspector gives last minute instructions to RTL1445's driver as the queue on Eccleston Bridge boards for a ride along the route mostly followed by the Queen's coronation procession in 1953. */ C. Carter*

Centre right: A range of tours was offered in Coronation year. RT1692 is about to set off on circular tour service J from the stretch of Buckingham Palace Road that was later to be used for southbound Green Line stops on their removal from Eccleston Bridge. */ C. Carter*

Below: The AEC Regal IV chassis in its 7ft 6in wide version was bodied by Metro-Cammell to become LT's RF type, 268 of which provided the bulk of Green Line services from 1951 onwards. Some of them were given a more modern appearance later on in life, like RF281, finally disposed of in autumn 1977. Route 701, Ascot to Gravesend, had gone two years before. */ J. G. S. Smith*

Right: A light blue double-deck bus in Buckingham Palace Road was an unusual event. London Country hired some Maidstone Corporation Leyland Titans and very occasionally one helped on a Green Line journey. The occasion here was motor racing at Brands Hatch. / *D. M. Persson*

Below: RT1106 acted as a Green Line relief on the 718 in the early 1970s. The travellers took advantage of the advertised bargains. The London Country winged wheel motif, applied to RTs on the staircase side, did not last for very long before National Bus livery superseded the Lincoln green of LCBS. / *J. G. S. Smith*

Above: Leyland Atlantean bus AN90 would have been more at home on a Harlow town service rather than relieving on the 718. This bus is the last in the first batch bodied by Park Royal Vehicles, and was delivered in National Bus livery in 1972.
/ D. M. Persson

Right: Arrival at the vague 'London' destination meant Eccleston Bridge for Routemaster coach RMC1499, back on Green Line duties after demotion to country bus work.
/ J. G. S. Smith

West End

The West End is an area almost impossible to define and where it starts and finishes must be left largely to individual opinion. It is certainly an area intensely concerned with work, leisure, and shopping and yet — despite still rising costs — it is desirable residentially. All this calls for public transport, which over the years regarding buses, has meant very many standard red double-deckers.

'Prewar' RT82 negotiates Marble Arch after the war. Though it has lost its rear wheels hub disc, the bus retains the nearside route number stencil. On postwar RTs this panel remained unused and painted red. / *S. A. Newman collection*

Above: Those who live at Buckingham Palace seldom have service buses passing their door. In September 1950 they had. Roadworks in Piccadilly meant diverting buses away from that street, and route 19's RTs circled the Queen Victoria Memorial. RT1250 had a Saunders body with the further back offside route number plate. / *C. Carter*

Right: Looking through a Routemaster's front windows to see an oncoming RCL on its way to Royal Windsor passing the Royal Albert Hall in summer 1967. / *John A. Gray*

719 HEMEL HEMPSTEAD LONDON 719
GREEN LINE
719 LONDON
GREEN LINE
LYF 426

GREEN LINE
716 HITCHIN
COACH STOP
LONDON COUNTRY
HEADACHE
PAY AS YOU ENTER
PLEASE
RF 619
NLE 619

Above left: Modernised RF75 heads south under a statue's feet in Edgware Road with the appearance its designer intended: Lincoln green with pale green band, gold fleet name and bullseye transfers and full painted side routeboards. / *J. G. S. Smith*

Left: For comparison, here's bus RF619 at Hyde Park Corner. It suffers from headache advertising and panel bashing. 'Nelly' 619 finished London Country life in April 1975. / *J. G. S. Smith*

Above: Contemporary Leyland National standards may not have improved noticeably since Green Line Routemaster and RF days, some regular travellers might say. Dented LNB69, really a bus, takes on few passengers at Marble Arch soon after delivery in 1973. / *J. G. S. Smith*

Right: Sovereign silver in Sloane Square. Properly RM1914 became SRM10 for 1977. / *C. Stannard*

Left: An AEC Regent formerly owned by East Kent Road Car Co also wore a silver coat of paint for the Queen's Silver Jubilee, though it was not in LT service. Here passengers could see the sights of Notting Hill Gate. / *C. Stannard*

Below: In about 1935, when the Monico site at Piccadilly Circus was still Monico's, STs, LTs, STLs and a former independent's Leyland Titan form their own queue to gain Regent Street. / *G. Robbins collection*

Right: More recently, ST922 turns up regularly on special route 100. This time in Pall Mall, the bus shows interestingly an offside route number stencil for the 12! / *Julian Bowden-Green*

Below right: A Guy Arab working for London Transport again: this former East Kent bus was used for a summer season on the sightseeing tour, starting here under Eros' wings. / *J. G. S. Smith*

Burberrys
Haymarket and Regent Street, London.
STRAND (LAW COURTS)
ST. PAUL'S CATHEDRAL
MONUMENT
LONDON TRANSPORT
GJ 2098

ROUND LONDON SIGHTSEEING TOUR
LONDON TRANSPORT
ROUND LONDON
FFN 378

Above: Dented RTL1472 moves smartly along Pall Mall. It was one of the first RTLs to enter service in a modified condition to reduce apparent engine vibration when idling. / *Don Morris*

Left: Route 7 (and its former companion 7A) has run through the northern part of the West End for a very long time. Square cab ST1101 must have been photographed on a very hot day in about 1950 to have had so many windows wide open. The bonnet side had been opened too, presumably to help cool the petrol engine.
/ *S. A. Newman collection*

Above: For a while Merlin MBA588 was painted in an experimental livery with white window surrounds additional to the usual white band. Here it is in Great Portland Street, before the flat 5p fare was doubled. / *J. G. S. Smith*

Right: Dawn greets night bus DMS747 on Edgware Road route N94 in Oxford Street. Until October 1960 the route had been numbered 294, but in company with the other 2XX sequence night routes, it was reduced by 200 and prefixed 'N' to make way for trolleybus conversion routes. / *J. G. S. Smith*

Top right: The People's League for the Defence of Freedom ran some buses of provincial origin like this Duple-bodied Daimler CWA6 during the 1958 busmen's strike. This former Lytham St Annes wartime bus picks up in Park Lane. / *D. W. K. Jones*

Centre right: There is a little author's licence to include this photograph, way out in the western end. Paddington Transport's Regal was once LT's T363 and was hired in 1949 to help on route 7A. Compared with the Whitehall picture of the same vehicle, it can be noticed that the bodywork has been modified in several ways: the front nearside has been squared up; sliding vents have replaced the louvred windows; it now has only a front door, and a flared skirt has replaced tucked under panelling. / *D. W. K. Jones*

Below: 1300AS was the last of eight Austin 1 ton vans delivered in 1963. It is endorsed 'Lifts and Escalators' on its door. The van was photographed at Marble Arch. / *Alan B. Cross*

Marylebone

Marylebone has the distinction of having several places in London's transport history. The New Road, as Marylebone Road was called by the Turnpike Trust that built it, was to be the limit of any incoming railway construction, according to an 1846 Royal Commission conclusion. Before that, in 1829, George Shillibeer opened the first London bus route along Marylebone Road, with terminals for the three-horse buses at Paddington Green and at the Bank in the City.

The first underground railway, the Metropolitan, was opened in 1863, to run from Paddington to Farringdon Street below ground — and under Marylebone Road. Baker Street station served Marylebone Road and the immediate growing area. A final distinction for Marylebone was the opening of the last main line railway terminus in London — the Great Central's station — in March 1899; it still kept to the north side of Marylebone Road as the 1846 Commission had decreed.

Both stations have been used as bus terminals and are important traffic exchange points for buses passing through. Neither station has the volume of bus-rail interchange of, say, London Bridge or Victoria. Marylebone has too few trains to encourage such use, and though Baker Street is incomparably busier, only a small proportion of the passengers transfers to or from bus or Green Line.

In the days when route 23 terminated at Marylebone station, wartime Guy G115 performed a duty from Barking garage. New in 1943, the bus had angular Park Royal bodywork and room enough under an extended bonnet for a six-cylinder Gardner diesel engine, though the five-cylinder version was fitted to all London Guys.
/ S. A. Newman collection

Left: Route 1 has been associated with Marylebone's turn of the century railway terminus for many years, though until more recent times it ran beyond into the north western suburbs. RT4355 squeezes through delicate ironwork in the private station approach. / *J. G. S. Smith*

Below: TF35c leaves Baker Street and crosses into Marylebone Road on route 714 to Dorking after Green Line's postwar resumption. / *S. A. Newman collection*

Right: More than 20 years later, RF43 crosses the same spot on route 716A to Woking, not that anyone would know its destination from the RMC indicator fitted to this revamped RF. / *J. G.S. Smith*

Below right: Round the back of Baker Street station in October 1939 stands an early Chiswick Works lorry, still with solid tyres. This AEC had been brought out of storage to help with war emergency duties, this time in evacuating equipment from LT's Baker Street offices to a less vulnerable place. / *D. W. K. Jones*

GREEN LINE
716A
Weybridge Kingston
London (Marble Arch)
Welham Grn. Welwyn Gdn City
CHICKEN INN
PAY AS YOU ENTER
PLEASE
LYF 394

LONDON TRANSPORT
EMERGENCY SERVICE
17
064 GH

Left: At the back of Baker Street station again, purpose-built Green Line coach Q230 prepares for the 714 run to Dorking in the late 1940s. The five clips in the roof side normally held a fully detailed route board. / *S. A. Newman*

Below : STDs growled their way along Baker Street for more than 20 years. STD34 basks in warm sunshine in the days when drivers wore a white crownpiece on their caps during the summer months. / *S. A. Newman collection*

Right: RT126 goes all continental with posters for the Latin Quarter production and spaghetti.
/ *S. A. Newman collection*

Below: With Chiltern Court flats, the nearest Metroland reached towards the City, in the background, STL2383 gets caught on route 27A in Marylebone Road's constant traffic. The bus was withdrawn in 1951 and was not one of the few from its batch to be reincarnated as an SRT.
/ *S. A. Newman collection*

Euston

Little can be said about today's Euston station, whose forecourt is used for terminating buses. The facade, built anew under British Rail's reconstruction programme for the whole station, attracts only one of the 77 group of routes to turn there and that might be termed as a part-time occupation. Nowadays just two other routes terminate at Euston station, one (170) a part-timer like the 77, and only 188 a daily adherent. It should, however, be recalled that regular use of the station as a terminus is very much a postwar development outside peak hours.

Top left: Leyland Cub one and a half deck C108 glows in the old Euston station while serving the nights-only interstation route. Much later in their lives these buses were operated as airport connection coaches by London Transport on BEA's behalf. / *S. A. Newman collection*

Bottom left: Merton garage has been associated with the 77 routes for a long while. RT4212's home was there. The bus was eventually withdrawn from service in February 1976. / *J. G. S. Smith*

Above right: A Routemaster leaves Euston Grove, in front of the station, in March 1977. RM1760 shows signs of oil fuel spillage as did the RT. Though having first to turn left, the signal flashes right preparatory to crossing traffic in Euston Road and turning right into Upper Woburn Place. / *John A. Gray*

Right: Soldier statuary appears to bow to SMS555, a Swift with Metro-Cammell 67-passenger capacity bodywork, in spring 1977. Euston is the furthest north route 188 now reaches. When introduced in July 1951 as an extended cover for tram 68, it went beyond, through Camden Town, to terminate at Chalk Farm. RTs worked it then. / *John A. Gray*

77
TOOTING MITRE
The new way to take your car to Spain.
EUSTON GROVE
760 DYE

LONDON TRANSPORT
red bus rovers

Holborn and Smithfield

In the wake of the trams the trolleybuses came to Holborn and to Smithfield. Smithfield was not in the borough of Holborn, as Bloomsbury was. All three areas can be taken together as the north western innermost trolleybus neighbourhoods.

Trolleys left Bloomsbury for ever in 1959 and the Holborn loop in 1961; and even Holborn as its own borough ceased to exist in the 1965 merger into Camden. *Camden* wouldn't have sounded right for trolleybuses.

Quiet at Smithfield. Leyland trolleybus 1698 stands deserted in May 1953. This class, P1, had MCW bodywork and was introduced in 1941, but still with prewar standards. London received no utility trolleys, only diverted South African orders. / *C. Carter*

Left: In negotiating the streets forming the Holborn turning loop, the routes numbered in the 600s went clockwise and the 500s anti-clockwise. In the short stretch of Charterhouse Street between Farringdon Road and Holborn Circus, a short terminal pause was made. The pausing leader in this 1953 picture is 313, an AEC with Birmingham RCW bodywork of the 1936 Class C3. Its nearside windscreen is a single fixed pane, though originally it had been openable, like the offside. */ C. Carter*

Below: AEC chassisless trolleybus 1456 of Class L3 turns in the narrow Bloomsbury side streets before heading back eastwards in March 1954. This class introduced route 665 when it took over from trams in June 1940. The compulsory bus stop flag in Parton Street carries the 'setting down point only' legend. */ C. Carter*

Above: Class L3 trolleybus No 1525 leaves Farringdon Street on the dismal final day of route 617, 1 February 1961. From the L classes onwards, all London's standard trolleybuses had the bodybuilders' interpretation of streamlining applied to the upper deck front windows. / *C. Carter*

Left: All-Leyland 1180 of Class K2 turns at Smithfield on the final day of route 679 in April 1961. / *C. Carter*

Top left: Trolley 1540 belonged to Class M1, of AEC unit construction lightweight chassis with the Board's own bodywork, and was delivered early in wartime. At the end of its life, 1540 and some classmates spent about six months on route 621 till it was withdrawn in November 1961. Here it was ready to turn from High Holborn, outside the restored Tudor style Staple Inn, into Gray's Inn Road. / *C. Carter*

Centre left: At Holborn Circus, the statue of Queen Victoria's husband, Prince Albert, raises a hat to 1514 working route 621's final day, 7 November 1961, 100 years after the Prince's death. A Routemaster follows on route 259 which replaced trolleybus route 659 some six months earlier. / *C. Carter*

Below: Motor buses run in Holborn too! Route 8 runs the full breadth of the old borough from St Giles Circus in the west to Staple Inn in the east, and beyond over Holborn Viaduct. This full height Eastern Coach Works-bodied Bristol K type helped out from Clay Hall garage in 1949 in its Eastern Counties red livery, giving it the edge over the green hired Bristols in wearing at least a closer likeness to central bus livery. / *C. Carter*

Right: Holborn reached to take in the northern end of Chancery Lane. This route 67 was withdrawn in 1958 and a few years later the street became one way only. RTL473 lasted on the books till the late 1960s. / *C. Carter*

Below: A very early morning shopper waits while RT4126 passes by on night route N98 at Holborn Circus / *J. G. S. Smith*

Finsbury Square

Finsbury Square, office-lined, lies just north of Moorgate. For trolleybuses it was convenient as a turning point for the vehicles coming from the north, but not as a terminus for their passengers. Many must surely have wished the trolleys had penetrated the City itself, but like the trams before them, they were never so allowed.

Motor buses in trolleybus days came to the Square from the opposite direction to turn there. Route 21 came from the depths of Kent; prewar it had run beyond the Square northwards over tram tracked Green Lanes to turn back at Turnpike Lane.

Top left: Tilling ST1027 imparts no intermediate route information as it waits departure time on route 21 to Sidcup from the Square. Royal London House was still shored up by massive timber buttresses anchored in the bomb-damaged gap. / *C. Carter*

Bottom left: This Leyland in C. G. Lewis's dark maroon and cream colours was one of the postwar coach hirings to have roller blinds in use. Edging in behind was LT210. / *J. F. Higham*

Above: Class C1 trolleybuses were the first of LT's standard types to seat 70 passengers. No 163 was an AEC with Metro-Cammell bodywork, modified somewhat at the front end early during its life by the insertion of a full width bulkhead behind the driver, a single pane nearside windscreen and the replacement of between decks sidelights (just discernible as a panelled slit in the front cream band by the driver's mirror mounting) by torpedo lights. The time of the picture is the early 1950s. / *S. A. Newman collection*

Left: Wood Green depot's trolleybus 844 heads the Finsbury Square line in March 1953. Class H1 was built by Leyland/MCW in 1937-38, and began to be withdrawn after the 5 per cent service reductions in 1958-59. / *C. Carter*

Right: Trolleybus 1364 leaves Moorgate terminus in Finsbury Square for the rustic-sounding Highgate Village on the 611 in May 1953. The 15-strong Class L1 to which 1364 belonged were stationed at Holloway depot for use on route 611 which negotiated the steep Highgate Hill. The trolleys had special braking devices to help prevent runaways on the gradient. / *C. Carter*

Below: For about six months before final conversion in 1961, trolleybus route 609 had the distinction of being partly worked by Routemasters. Finchley depot continued with trolleys while Highgate used, among others, RM589, here leaving the Square some eight years later than the previous photograph. / *C. Carter*

Right: Sparklingly new RML891 pulls out past engineering vehicles and staff engaged already on dismantling trolleybus equipment on the day buses took over route 609 as 104 on 8 November 1961. The RML's grilles beneath the headlamps have since been panelled in. This was the first time route information was displayed in the capital initials and lower case letters style. The tower wagon was AEC Mercury, No 82Q in the service vehicles fleet, and behind, 953B was a Perkins-engined Bedford-Scammell 8 ton articulated low-loader. / *Modern Transport*

Below: Sidcup's RT2676 looks glad to have a rest as steam escapes. RM983 from New Cross also on route 21 shows the plainer fleetname without underlining. / *J. G. S. Smith*

Shoreditch

Shoreditch is a forgotten district immediately outside the northern boundary of the City of London. It has industrial activity hardly of the City's kind: it is a place to pass through quickly on the way to and from the City. Most buses do just that; but the church has been a terminus for two bus routes that for many years have come from south of the Thames — probably the first convenient terminus they could reach after passing through the City and by the markets and small factories in which many of their peak-hour passengers worked.

Charles W. Banfield's mid-green Leyland Tiger coach was hired to run postwar on Shoreditch church's route 78 to Dulwich in south London. During the hire, the Essex-registered vehicle was operated from Nunhead garage, later to house the Banfield fleet. / *J. F. Higham*

Left: Coming to more recent times on route 78, RM1425 sports the rather shortlived bullseye fleetname on the side. / *J. G. S. Smith*

Below: Class K2 all-Leyland trolleybus 1161 on route 649 leads similar Class K1 member 1073 on route 557 northwards into Shoreditch High Street. While route 649 continued along the same alignment far out to Waltham Cross, the 557 trolley was shortly to turn right into Hackney Road and follow a less straightforward journey across the Lea Valley to Chingford Mount. The two buses were almost the same apart from the manufacture of electrical equipment; one detail difference was in the rows of louvres in the lower front panelling. / *Don Morris*

Above: Shoreditch High Street in 1968 and a Leyland RT leads an AEC one. RTL1574 has a long journey in front of it into far-off Kent. The RT's journey to Clapham was shorter but the journey would have started back at Chingford Hatch, though later in the year its terminus was switched to Hackney. / *J. G. S. Smith*

Right: Route 8A is a useful link from London Bridge station through the eastern part of the City to the East End. RM2114 with an interior-lit offside advertisement leaves what must be one of London's tiniest streets regularly used by service buses, Holywell Lane, to cross Shoreditch High Street and so gain Bethnal Green Road. / *J. G. S. Smith*

Aldgate

On the eastern fringe of the City of London, Aldgate was the terminus for trolleybus routes radiating along the Whitechapel and Commercial Roads into the densely populated East End. Minories runs down to the Tower, and at its northern end was built the bus and coach station, on a roof above the Aldgate junction of the Underground railway lines. It was opened about six months before the outbreak of World War II and was immediately a useful and busy terminus for trolleybuses, Green Line coaches and buses alike. Today it is much less busy; the trolleys have gone and the bus services that replaced them have been cut from time to time. Only one Green Line route now runs in, compared with a postwar peak of seven all-year routes and one seasonal. There is indeed now room for its use as a picking-up and setting-down point for longer-distance coach services.

Class N2 chassisless trolleybus 1667 with Park Royal bodywork waits to leave Minories. The picture dates from before late 1950, when trolleybus depots were coded in the manner of bus garages: here the trolley merely carries its white on black running number. This particular bus has only three opening windows per side, two fewer than usual. / *S. A. Newman collection*

Above: Underfloor-engined TF36 has wheels turned ready to leave on the northbound Green Line route 720 to Bishop's Stortford in 1953.
/ T. W. Moore

Right: Daimlers were associated with Aldgate's Green Lines in the early postwar period. D176 entered service in 1946 with this Duple bodywork. The buses — for in no sense could they be termed coaches — were in green livery and worked from Romford garage, Country Bus area.
/ S. A. Newman

HEINZ
tomato soup
PERSIL
washes
whiter!
JOHN CLIFFORD
GOWNS
LITTLEWOODS
VP
wines
567
BARKING
KIT-E-KAT
FXH 486

GREEN LINE
722
UPMINSTER
KYY964

Above left: When British wine cost six shillings a bottle, Class L3 trolleybus enters the bus station on route 567 which was to be supplanted by new bus route 5 in November 1959. / *Don Morris*

Left: New RTs in Green Line livery took over from the Daimlers; in 1953, RT3235 stands reflecting the return from Minories to Corbets Tey on the 722. / *Don Morris*

Above: Route 653 followed an inverted U course from Minories round to Tottenham Court Road, though trolleybus 1025, an AEC/MCW of Class J2, indicates a short working. In 1950, this short part of the route had an advertised two-to-three minute frequency. / *Don Morris*

Below: Bus route 253 took over from the 653 in February 1961, and continued much the same but on a reduced frequency when this picture of an almost empty Aldgate was taken in April 1978. RM496 coming in on 253 pauses for the picture while, broadside, RM877 takes a rest on a route 25 short working. The background has changed dramatically in the 25-year gap between the two photographs. / *John A. Gray*

Above: RM504 shows that Finsbury Park shorts were worked on route 253 too, here joined by RTL1597. The Leyland bus left the LT fleet early in 1970 at about the time route 40 changed its north of Thames destination from Wanstead to East Ham. / *J. G. S. Smith*

Left: Early RM183 stands almost alone in January 1966 ready for route 40B, a number to disappear later that year. / *J. G. S. Smith*

Above right: Between September 1968 and January 1970, Red Arrow route 501 served Aldgate bus station. Seated in the low position, the driver of MBA29 looks around to the passenger using the turnstile. Soon afterwards this bus was to be reseated to join the MB type. / *J. G. S. Smith*

Right: Driver and inspector chat near to RT2211's engine warmth on a cold day, while behind, the back indicator of RMC1476 shows a return Green Line journey to Tilbury, and on the right, RM94 shows shapely legs. / *J. G. S. Smith*

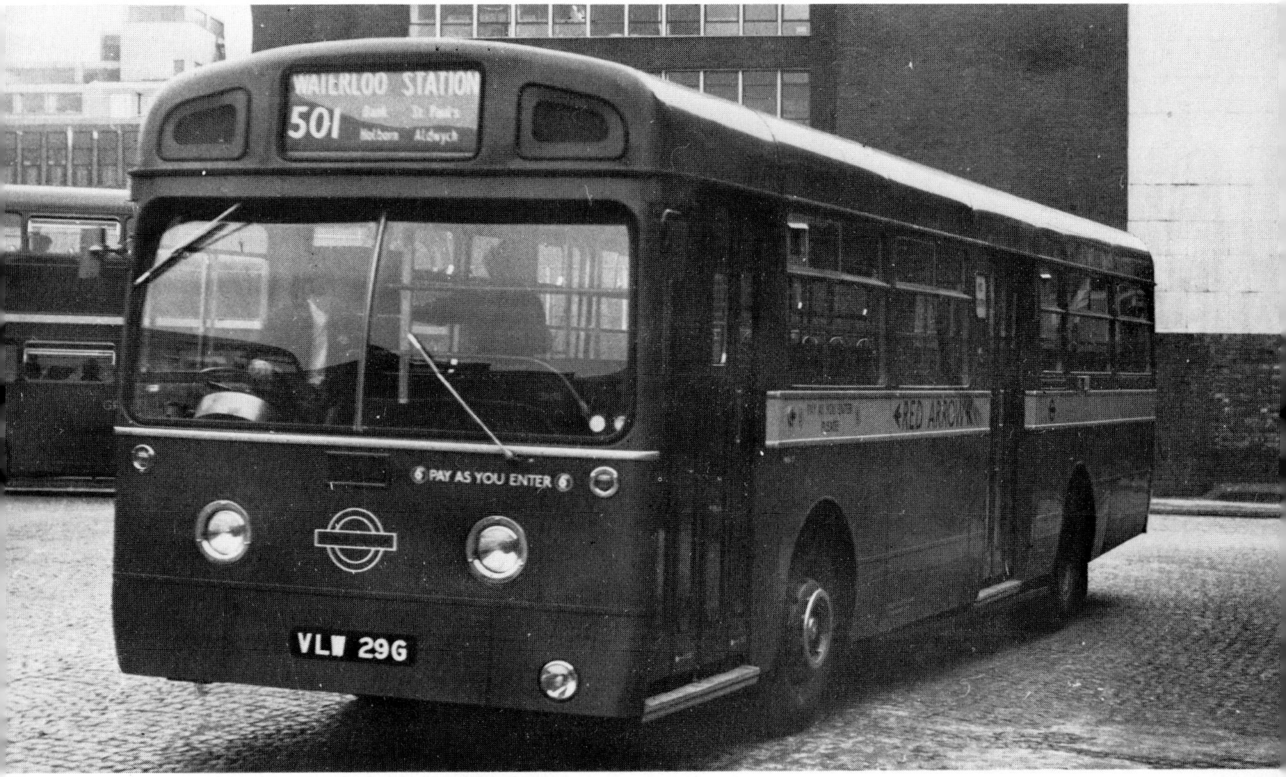

WATERLOO STATION
501
RED ARROW
PAY AS YOU ENTER
VLW 29G

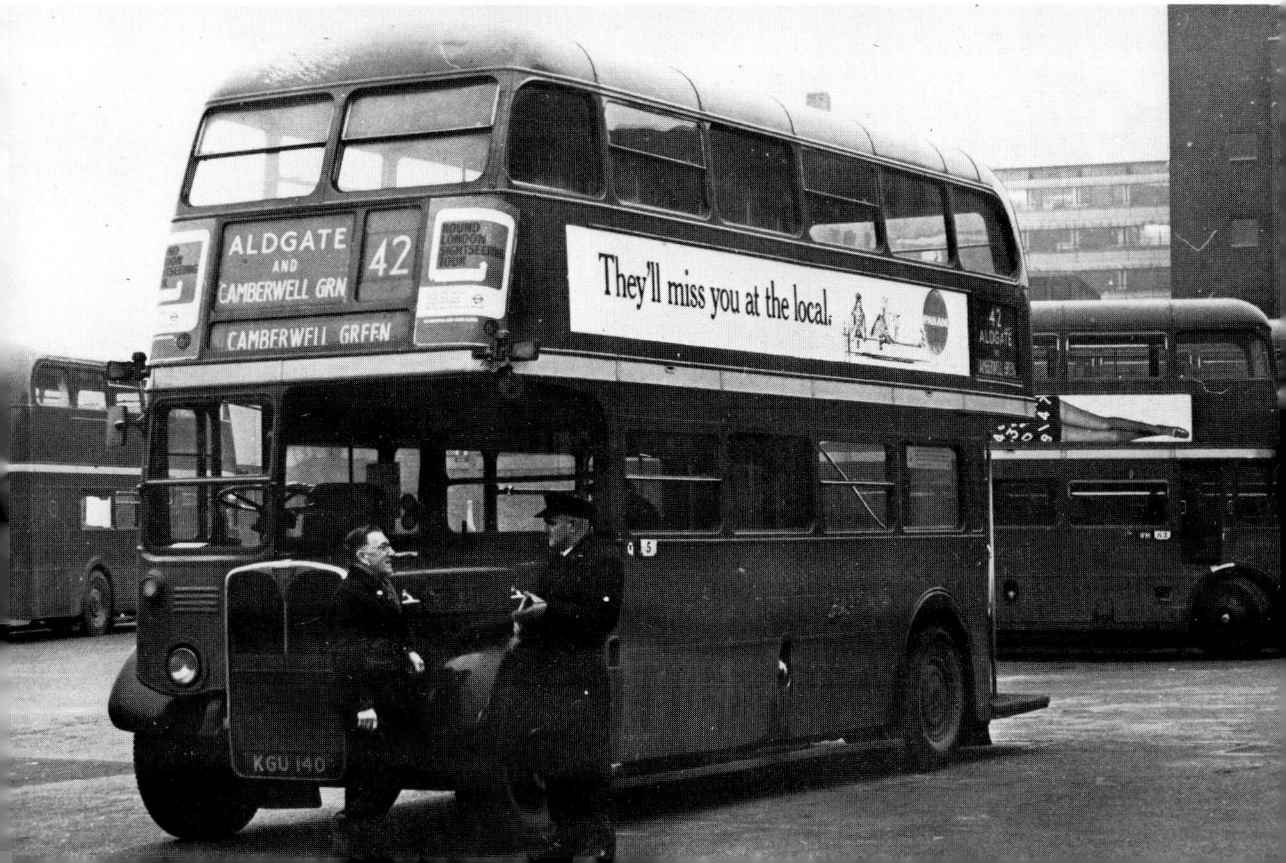

ALDGATE
AND
CAMBERWELL GRN
42
CAMBERWELL GREEN
ROUND LONDON SIGHTSEEING TOUR
They'll miss you at the local.
PANAM
KGU 140

Top right: Still very new in January 1966 long Routemaster coach RCL2242 shows its rather bland fleetnames treatment, when compared with some of its predecessors. Now, with a new level of comfort, the double-deck Green Line vehicles from Aldgate could properly be called coaches. / *J. G. S. Smith*

Centre right: Four buses have turned to take up their layover stances in Minories, April 1978: one Fleetline, whose popular name 'Londoner' never caught on, and three Routemasters, whose did. / *John A. Gray*

Below: Only one Green Line route terminated at Minories by April 1978. Leyland National SNC118 leaves for its home garage town of Grays on route 723. One concession to comfort made in this 'coach' is the provision of high-backed seats. However, anyone of short stature would still find it hard to see out when sitting in the forward low-placed seats — as demonstrated here. / *John A. Gray*

Tower of London and Tower Bridge

Protecting the River Thames entrance to the City at the eastern end, the Tower of London has had a bus route passing its moated front door only in more recent times — and then, until October 1978, only on Sundays, to carry sightseers. Two routes have, for a much longer period, run regularly along the Tower's eastern flank, between it and that other royal institution, the Mint.

These two routes cross over that example of late Victorian engineering, Tower Bridge. The roadway is carried on bascules which are capable of being raised very quickly — considering their size and weight — to allow tall shipping to pass at high tide. It's an experience to sit at the front of a double-deck bus waiting at the traffic lights while the bascules are raised and lowered, and a thrill to feel the gentle bump as the bus passes over the meeting bascules, while looking across to London's river and the City's fortified entrance at the Tower.

Route 9A ran on Sundays past the Tower of London, until October 1978, a facility introduced no doubt with the visitors in mind who are now catered for by the daily 9. RM150 passes nearby indicating its fairly long garage journey back to Dalston. */ J. G. S. Smith*

Above: The Tower district has many famous buildings. One of them is the Royal Mint at East Smithfield shown as the background to DMS2108 about to pass on to the approach to Tower Bridge in early spring 1978. / *John A. Gray*

Below: In March 1963, RT750 leaves the southern side of Tower Bridge, whose traffic lights seem more recently to be almost permanently at green, now that so little tall shipping needs to pass at high tide. Route 78 has wound its way to a Dulwich terminus since well before the war. / *C. Carter*

Right: RM1333 is a member of the succeeding generation of 78s going southbound, despite the indication. / *J. G. S. Smith*

Far right: Rear-engined single-decker gives way to rear-engined double-decker. Daimler DMS2104 leaves the 20mph restriction imposed for the bascule part of the bridge on a southwards route 42 journey to Camberwell in April 1978. The crenellated superstructure of the bridge complements the roofline of the Tower itself, peeping through on the left. / *John A. Gray*

Newsweek
HISTORY IN THE MAKING
42
CAMBERWELL GREEN
Newsweek
THE WORLD AT A GLANCE
KJD104P
20
FOOTWAY
AHEAD
CLOSED
CROSS HERE

London Bridge and Southwark

London Bridge was the first to span the Thames and the original one did so, repaired and altered, from medieval times till replaced by the second bridge, opened in 1831. When this second one ended its London life by 1970, it was dismantled and most of it reused in a newly-built structure at Lake Havasu in south-western USA.

Southwark grew up on the Surrey bank at the southern end of London Bridge. Londoners used to refer to the place simply as 'the Borough'. The first London railway terminus was opened in 1836 in the Borough near to the bridge, whose name it took. Later, the station became a tram, and then more particularly a bus centre. The forecourt of the station keeps its use for buses. It has been roofed over for the first time as part of a major reconstruction of the whole station.

Prewar panorama of London Bridge and the City. An ST leads a route 69 STL over the old bridge, built in 1831 and widened early in this century.

Above: Early postwar now and LT29 of the first variant with open staircase gets caught in heavy traffic in beginning to cross the Thames from the City bank. / *S. A. Newman*

Right: STL57 had progressed only a little further on to the bridge. This Tilling type had the unusual arrangement of three upper deck front windows, the centre one of which could be opened. The eye posters succeeded in attracting attention. / *S. A. Newman*

Left: One of 11 wartime Leyland Titan TD7s, STD106 starts northbound across the bridge soon after the war. Both it and the LT behind carry the eyelash posters of a competing journal. / *S. A. Newman*

Below: DM1099 on route 40 runs past the same spot as the STD about 30 years on, in 1978. The bridge, the third here, will have to endure if it is to outlive the first, which lasted for six centuries. The towers of Cannon Street station and St Paul's Cathedral dome are about to be obscured by the Daimler. / *John A. Gray*

Above: While the Maudslay coach of C. G. Lewis, Greenwich, on route 21 all but nudges the policeman on point duty, an inspector holds his hand up to the driver of an ST on route 8A. Coach and bus arrive in Southwark after crossing London Bridge in 1949. / *J. F. Higham*

Right: Two 'quiet' Fleetlines with Leyland B20 engines rest under roof construction work at London Bridge bus station in April 1978. The 'tv screen' reflection central in the bustle window is caused by a wide angle reversing glass for driver's use. Both buses have Metro-Cammell bodywork; the front one has the newly-introduced 'T' shape offside advertisement using the staircase panelling. / *John A. Gray*

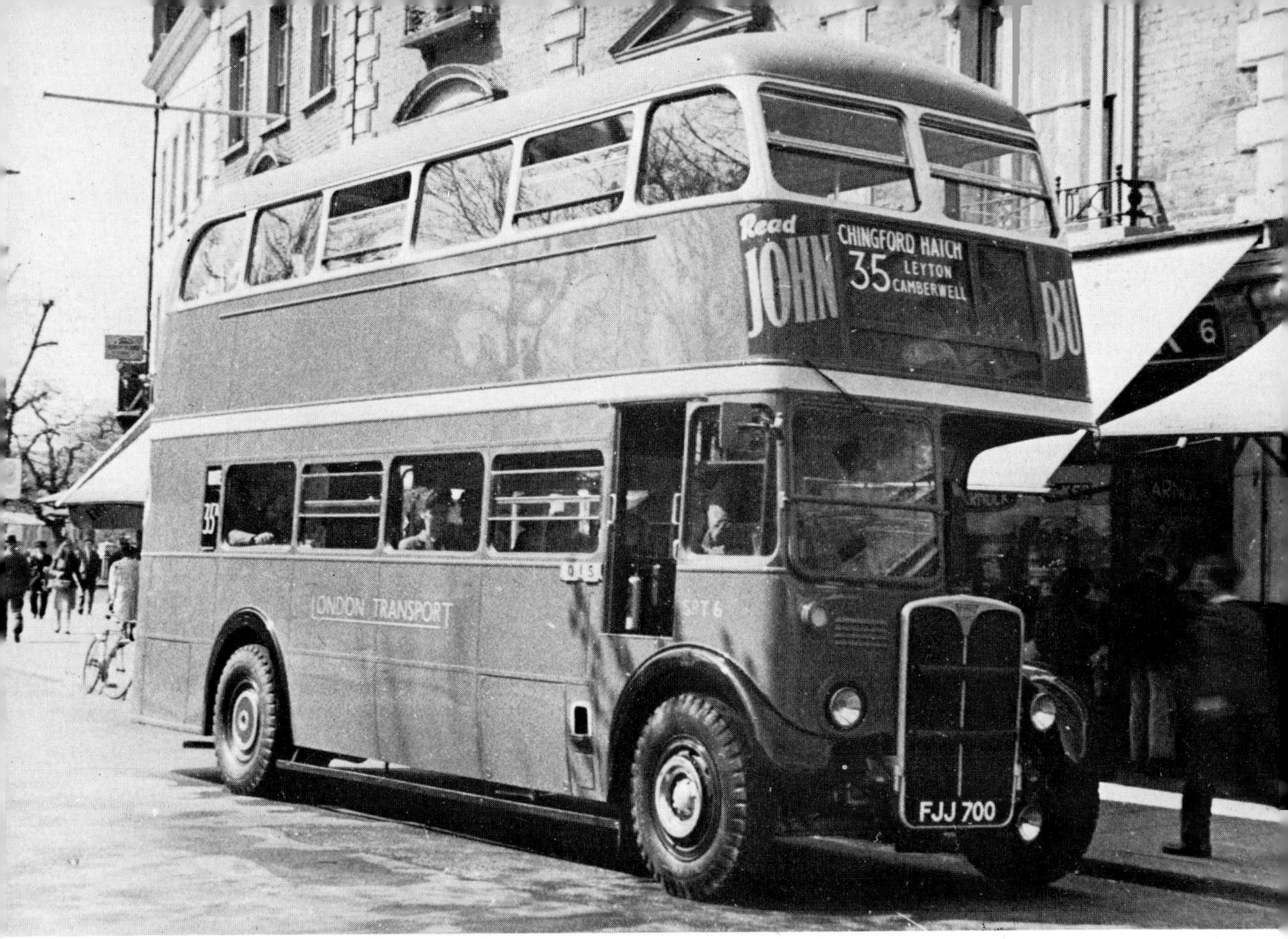

Read JOHN BU
CHINGFORD HATCH
35 LEYTON CAMBERWELL
LONDON TRANSPORT
SRT 6
FJJ 700

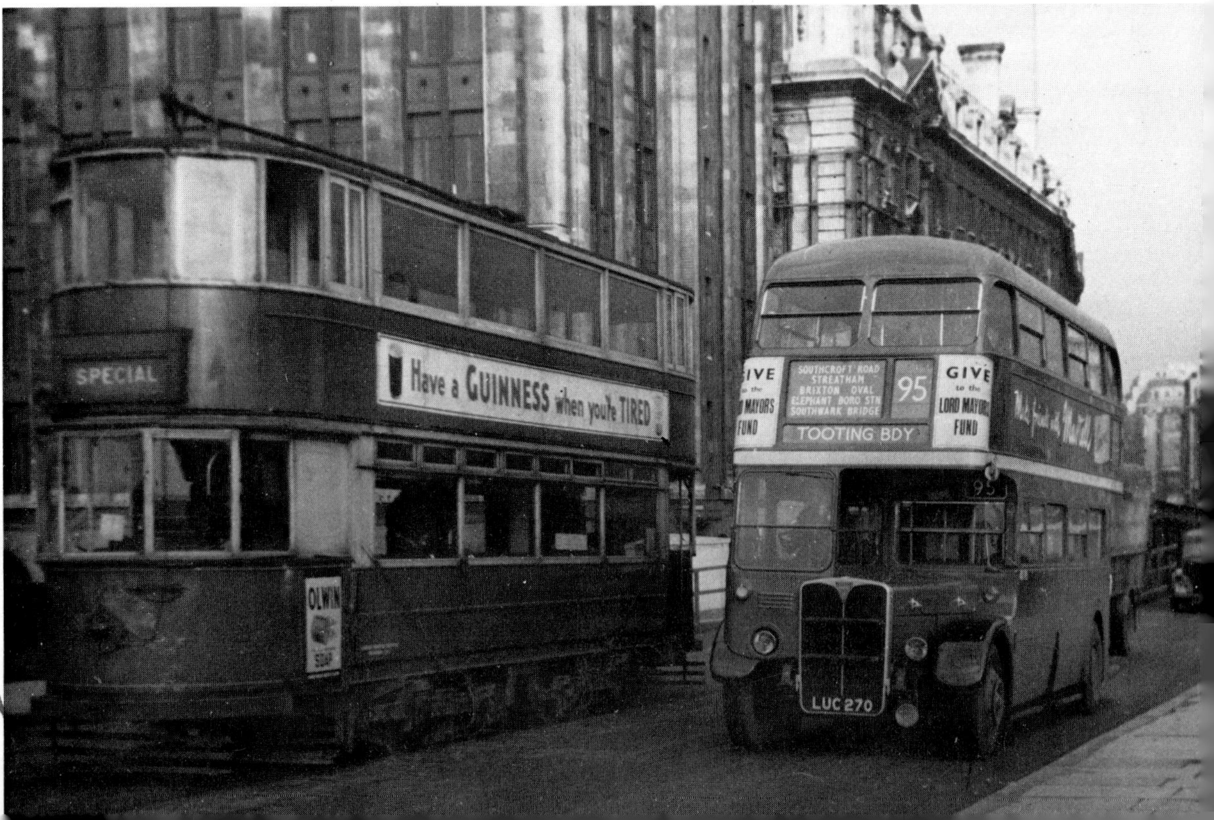

SPECIAL
Have a GUINNESS when you're TIRED
OLWIN SOAP
GIVE to the LORD MAYORS FUND
SOUTHCROFT ROAD STREATHAM BRIXTON OVAL ELEPHANT BORO' STN SOUTHWARK BRIDGE
95
TOOTING BDY
LUC 270

Left: New, with few advertisements and clearly the wall-ribbed tyres of the era, conversion SRT6 moves off in Southwark despite a running customer. The STL front wheel hubs were one of the few visual clues to ancestry of these buses; but listened to, their smaller 7.7 litre engines clearly distinguished them from their RT cousins.

Below left: Bus route 95 took over from tram route 10 in January 1951, and the two forms of transport were to share Southwark Bridge for the next 18 months till the last trams succumbed. RT2088 passes tram 1833 in the opposite direction. / *C. Carter*

Above: MBS166 runs in Tooley Street, Southwark, showing Tanner Street as destination. This Merlin sailed the seas to a new home in Australia in 1976. / *J. G. S. Smith*

Below: Hardly anyone left this evening aboard SMS61 in Southwark Street for the last portion of the journey along Stamford Street to Waterloo. The Borough was an inner London area where the two versions of AEC's rear-engined buses for LT could be seen operating alongside. The 2ft 7in difference in length is so well-camouflaged as to be barely discernible. More easily noticed on this Swift are its paired foglamps and painted below-window beading, compared with the Merlin's single lamp and aluminium strip. / *J. G. S. Smith*

Waterloo

Never a bus terminal centre in the way of either London Bridge or Victoria, Waterloo began to catch up some lost time when many of the short distance Red Arrow routes were introduced to terminate, some within the station precincts. An earlier period of bus popularity for this main line station was during the Festival of Britain 1951 celebrations. The South Bank site was only across the road — York Road — and frequent special services were operated throughout the festivity period. An altered Royal Festival Hall remains as the only period reminder of the many structures especially built for the celebrations.

On a bright day in June 1951, STL1658 picks up in York Road amidst the Festival of Britain celebrations. Elderly STLs had been saved for use on the routes — for once officially termed 'services' — A to H. / *D. W. K. Jones*

Above: Only two years before, LT was hiring vehicles. This bright green AEC Regal belonged to W. P. Julius of Porson Street, Lewisham, having originally been with the London Co-operative Society, and was used on route 1. Here it waits outside Waterloo main line station. / *J. F. Higham*

Centre right: A little way along Waterloo Road 20 years later in April 1969 and RML2751 passes RT3779. Very near this spot in the middle of the road was the terminal stand of route 68 trams, which were replaced by bus route 188. Coincidentally, tram route 68 met bus route 68 here. / *Edward Shirras*

Bottom right: When tram route 70 was withdrawn in July 1951, its replacement bus route of the same number was extended beyond the tram's Borough terminus in Tooley Street to Waterloo on weekdays. A later generation of buses to run on old tram routes was the one-man crew single-deck type exemplified by SMS361, here in Waterloo Road. Double-deckers have since taken over again. / *J. G. S. Smith*

Above: With high driving position, MBA529 on the Red Arrow shuttle route 503 overtakes RM1073 on the long 171 route in York Road, Waterloo: May 1976. / *C. Stannard*

Right: Back to the days when prewar buses still served on route 68, STL1552 leaves Lancaster Place past Somerset House and crosses first the Victoria Embankment which Waterloo Bridge spans in addition to London's river: March 1950. / *R. E. Vincent*

Thames Side

Much of the north bank of the Thames, from Blackfriars Bridge to Battersea Bridge, was the accomplishment of the Metropolitan Board of Works in the 1860s. The Victoria Embankment from Blackfriars to Westminster Bridge was built with the District Railway beneath it on the reclaimed river mudbank, and till the early 1950s it was the scene of a constant procession of trams. The trams never penetrated the dense areas of Whitehall and Charing Cross, but the replacing buses, with their greater flexibility of routeing, were able to deviate from the Embankment better to serve passengers' requirements elsewhere.

Further west, Pimlico retains the air of a private estate, even to the loop of terminating bus routes, serving the area developed in early Victorian times.

Waterloo Bridge, and above it, Somerset House, form the background to this 1951 view of the Victoria Embankment in the short period of parallel tram and bus operation. The tram on route 35, going away from the photographer, was about to turn off its reservation and across the main streams of Embankment traffic to burrow beneath the archway of the bridge and into the Kingsway Subway on route to the northern heights of indicated Highate, though in fact stopping short at the foot of Highgate Hill at Archway station. The approaching RTL1088 is on the 155. This route used suffix letters B and W for a short while on introduction to distinguish which way round the Embankment loop the bus would proceed according to which Thames bridge was met first — Blackfriars or Westminster / *C. Carter*

Left: Later times and perhaps evidence of declining patronage as RT684 runs along the Victoria Embankment, which by now had had the tram reservation removed to assume the appearance of a normal, if very wide, street. / *J. G. S. Smith*

Below: With National Bus Co. standard style fleetnames applied, RMC1499 soaks up the evening sun as it heads home to Godstone past Charing Cross railway bridge on the last day of two-member crew operation of Green Line route 709 in May 1976. / *C. Stannard*

Above: When vans had running boards — drivers could recline on them. LT's Commercial Advertising Department's Morris Commercial vans M28, M33 and M32 wait by the handy refreshment stall at Charing Cross Underground station in 1939. */ D. W. K. Jones*

Right: DMS270 picks up at the then Charing Cross Underground station, later Embankment, in 1974, on the bus route that replaced trams 36 and 38. */ J. G. S. Smith*

Above: RF187, once a Green Line coach, finds itself back on its old kind of duty even though by now relegated to bus status. Evidence can be seen in the roof curve of the clips which held the Green Line route boards, as the vehicle runs along Millbank in the early 1970s. / *J. G. S. Smith*

Left: Southwards and round the Thames curve to Pimlico, where in Lupus Street in 1933, soon after the LPTB's formation, waited this former British Automobile Traction AEC NS type on route 24. Solid-tyred buses like this were withdrawn as soon as possible. / *D. W. K. Jones*

Above: Forerunners of the Daimler Londoners were batches of Daimler Fleetlines and Leyland Atlanteans in the XF and XA types. They tested the principles of large capacity, rear engine and front entrance combined in a single design. Bodywork for both was built by Park Royal Vehicles. Route 24 was one of the first to try the new type; here, XA11 was caught in Pimlico. By 1973, all 50 buses of the XA type were sold for service in Hong Kong by London Transport and London Country. / *J. G. S. Smith*

Left: One of Leyland's B15 prototypes leaves the King William IV public house in Pimlico; it was just visible in the NS picture. Route 24 has seen some changes in 50 years evolution of bus design . . . / *J. G. S. Smith*

Scrap

London Transport seldom dismantles its own retired vehicles. They are usually sold to dealers throughout the country who remove them from LT's premises and take them to bits on their own premises. Sometimes a little more life is eked out of the worthy vehicles and they are resold for this purpose, but more likely than not, they are stripped of those parts which have a recovery value and the rest is burned.

Increasingly over the last 20 years there has been enthusiasm for preserving some of the more notable vehicles, and many of these are kept proudly by their new owners as living mementoes of London's past bus fleet.

STLs 352, 1753 and 838 and former Green Line T470 await their doom in about 1954. / *Don Morris*

Above: STD3 stands at the head of the column of prewar Leyland Titans looking tired after about 17 years' hectic work in London. / *Don Morris*

Right: Awaiting disposal, wartime STD102 still displays evidence of having been used as a training bus. / *Don Morris*

Right: Some STLs found useful employment after leaving LT's ownership. W. & C. French, the civil engineering contractor, employed identifiable STLs 948 and 1647 among others in the early 1950s. */ Don Morris*

Below: Breakdown tender 833J awaits disposal in August 1966 sandwiched between two dismantled RTWs at Aldenham Works. The lorry, used for railway emergencies throughout the inner city and other areas, had been converted from STL159 some 15 years earlier. */ Alan B. Cross*